I0023082

D. H. Howard

A Collection of Poems

D. H. Howard

A Collection of Poems

ISBN/EAN: 9783744704854

Printed in Europe, USA, Canada, Australia, Japan

A COLLECTION

OF

POEMS,

BY

D. H. HOWARD.

PREFACE.

The collection of Poems here presented to the public, has been made at the solicitation of friends. The author would have been glad of the assistance of some better literary judgment than his own, in the selection or rejection of articles, and for the correction of faults which may have escaped his own partial eye. Having been unable to enjoy this advantage, he feels that he has some right to claim the indulgence and clemency of the critic. Although he has been encouraged to think, from the commendation which many of these pieces have heretofore received, that they have some merit and value, he does not aspire after fame, nor seek to compete with great names. He will be satisfied, if he has succeeded in giving some innocent enjoyment, and still better, instruction, to such readers as his book may find, and in winning the approval of those who love the truth.

A BRIEF SKETCH OF THE AUTHOR'S LIFE.

The Author was born in Mansfield, Bristol County, Mass., in the year 1814. His early childhood was spent partly in Norton and partly in Mansfield; but since his tenth year, he has resided most of the time in North Bridgewater, (now Brockton), Plymouth County, Mass., his father's native place. He learned to read early, and was fond of reading, but never attended school before the age of eight years. Having attracted some attention by his early taste for poetical composition, he was assisted to nearly five years of gratuitous education, by Mrs. Ann McLean, a benevolent lady of Boston: first under the care of the late Jesse Pierce, of Stoughton: next, two weeks at the Boston Latin School, further progress being interrupted by illness; then three years at the Mount

Pleasant Classical Institution, in Amherst, Mass. Here he became acquainted with the Greek, Latin and French languages, and a very little Spanish. To these he afterwards added some knowledge of German, and still later, of Hebrew.

The year after leaving school, at the age of nineteen, he entered the printing office of William Pierce, in Boston. About six months after, he was engaged to work for George W. Light, another well known printer and publisher in that city, in whose employ he continued for several years. It was during his residence here that he first met with the writings of Swedenborg. His employer had taken the library of a debtor as security for a bad debt; and among these books were some of the writings of Swedenborg. Curiosity led the author to examine them, in spite of the superstitious fear he had been accustomed to entertain for them. Further reading, with much study and reflection, at length convinced him that they contained a correct explanation of the doctrines of Christianity. In the year 1839, the author left the printing office, on account of weak eyes. He was afterwards employed in the printing office of the Old Colony Reporter, published by T. D. Stetson, in North Bridgewater; and of the North Bridgewater Gazette, published by George Phinney in the same town. He also wrote occasionally for these two papers.

In 1845, the author began to write for the New Jerusalem Magazine, then published in Boston, and continued to do so from year to year, till its suspension in 1872. He also contributed articles to the New Church Children's Magazine, during its publication in Boston. He has also been a regular contributor to the New Jerusalem Messenger, since its establishment in New York, in 1855.

For quite a number of years he has been too much of an invalid to allow him to engage in any kind of business, and has been for most of the time confined at home by ill health. During this time, his only useful occupation has been the small amount of writing he was able to do, sometimes with his own hand, and sometimes by dictation. Having never been married, he has kept house with his sister since the death of his father and mother.

THE PARABLE OF LOVE.

A MARRIAGE POEM.

"The blossoming before fruit corresponds to the state of that age when the conjugial principle enters the mind, and gladdens it, thus when truth is conjoining to good; but fruit corresponds to the good itself, which so far as it ripens like fruit, so far it puts itself forth into works."—*Swedenborg's Arcana Cœlestia, No.* 10,185.

WOULDST thou understand the reason
Why Love's dear and blissful season,
Blooming with the sweetest flowers
Ever culled in earthly bowers,
With a more celestial glow
Sunned, than other seasons know,
Yields so soon to chilling frost,
All its bloom and beauty lost?
Why the holiest vow that's spoken
Is so oft, so rashly broken,
And the cords that ought to bind
Heart to heart and mind to mind

In the fondest union, prove
Chains of hate instead of love?
Learn a parable set forth
In the blossoms of the earth,
In their beauty half revealing,
In their bosoms deep concealing,
Heavenly secrets for the eyes
Of the pure in heart and wise.

—

When the May-wind, softly breathing
  Through the budding orchard trees,
Opens every nectared blossom
  To the honey-loving bees;

When the balmy air is laden
  All around with sweet perfume,
And the sun pours golden beauty
  Over Nature's bridal bloom;

Thou may'st wish the vernal glory
  Always to enchant thine eyes,
Through the summer, fresh and fragrant,
  Like the trees of Paradise.

Fool! to dream of heaven's fruition
  When its dawn is just begun!
Bread of Paradise is gathered
  Not till earthly work is done.

Spring-time bloom is but the promise
  Of a blessing yet to come;
Weary summer toils await thee,
  Ere thou bring the harvest home.

Soon a rougher gale will shatter
  All the orchard's blooming show,
And the snowy petals scatter
  Withered on the ground below.

But the wonder-work of Nature,
  In the vernal bud begun,
Still goes on in secret chambers,
  Cherished by the warming sun.

Quickly ope the spring-time blossoms:
  Soon their beauty fades away.
Slowly, 'mid the green leaves hiding,
  Very slowly, day by day,

Grows the fruit for Autumn's garners,
  Gathering from each summer shower,
From each warm and ripening sunbeam,
  Sweetness for the harvest hour.

And the toilsome farmer daily
  Lends to Nature kindly aid;
And with Autumn's fruitful treasures,
  Finds his care is well repaid.

Here behold, as in a mirror,
  What the angel, Love, demands,
Ere thou find his golden fruitage
  Ripened for thy waiting hands.

Life hath, like the year, its seasons:
  Like a tree, man grows and bears
In youth's freshness, lovely blossoms;
  Wisdom's fruit in manhood's years.

Marriage joy is spring-time blooming,
  Full of promise, full of hope;
Drink its wine of heavenly blessing,
  But beware thou break the cup.

And forget not, in the dreaming
  Of Love's joyous morning hour,
Why he crowns with purple blossoms
  And fresh leaves youth's virgin bower:

Why he pours the golden sunshine
  Into each dear blossom's heart,
Painting each unfolding petal,
  Quickening every inmost part.

Not for beauty's sake is beauty;
  Not to charm the wondering eye
With an idle show of splendor,
  Soon to fade away and die;

But a token and a promise
  Of a blessing hid within—
Good immortal, which the patient
  And the wise shall find and win.

Soon the storms of life will shatter
  Thy fond dreams of bliss and love,
And the painted blossoms scatter
  Torn and withered from the grove.

But behind his leafy curtains,
  When the bloom has passed away,
Love hides precious fruits to ripen,
  Through the golden summer day.

Ye whom he hath called together,
  Sealed your foreheads with his kiss,
Given to taste the heaven-rained manna
  Of his morning hour of bliss,

He hath put the sacred keeping
  Of his treasures in your care;
Ye must labor in his vineyard,
  If his blessings ye would share:

Lest the gales that strew the blossoms,
  Rend the ripening fruit away;
Lest the canker worm and locust
  Make it an untimely prey;

Lest a treacherous moth find entrance,
And its tender heart devour;
Chilling frost or blasting mildew
Smite it in an evil hour.

Tremble lest the harvest morning
Prove you faithless to your trust;
All his purple clusters blasted,
All his wheat-sheaves black with rust.

Love walks hand in hand with duty,
Wisdom follows in his train.
Would'st thou know his wondrous beauty?
His reward dost wish to gain?

Never let the present seeming
Cheat thy sense with gay deceit;
Let not summer's rosy pleasure,
Turn from duty's path thy feet.

Earth for careful toil yields blessings.
To the willing hand and heart;
But the idle dreamer findeth
Only blossoms for his part.

Costly gifts ask patient waiting;
Golden harvests, weary toil;
Only they who bravely conquer
In the battle, share the spoil.

Love has sown within your bosoms
  Gardens rich with plants of joy;
In your hearts arise the tempests
  That his vines and figs destroy.

As the shepherd wages warfare
  With the wolves that tear his sheep,
As the farmer with a thousand
  Foes that fly and foes that creep,

So shall ye give battle daily
  To the fiends that mar and sever
Household peace and heartfelt union,
  Binding soul to soul forever.

Angry strife and selfish passion,
  Cankering envy, stubborn pride,
Fiercer beasts than wolves and tigers;—
  How can love with these abide?

Drive the demons from your dwelling,
  While your hands are strong to fight;
Banish from beneath your roof-tree
  Every hateful bird of night.

In their places let fond ring-doves
  Under olive garlands play;
While gay linnets chirp sweet love-songs
  To the dawning summer day.

Shall not else the heavenly angel
  Sadly flee away in haste,
From the heart he once had hallowed;
  Leave it dark and cold and waste?

Nay, entreat him that he tarry.
  Deem no guest so dear as he:
In the brightest sunrise chamber
  Let his place of resting be.

Scatter India's choicest spices
  Where he lays his golden head;
Let soft curtains hang in purple
  Folds above his downy bed.

Wake him with the gladdest music
  Of the summer morning grove:
Let no sweet caress be wanting
  To the evening rest of Love.

Sharon's flocks and Bashan's fatlings
  Furnish dainties for his meat;
Milk of kine and comb of honey;
  Bread, the finest of thy wheat.

Wine of Lebanon for his drinking
  Golden goblets shall afford;
Ripest fruits of every season
  Heap upon the generous board.

O, let not your hands be weary
With a single month of care,
For the heaven-descended seraph
Ye have bid your home to share.

But with mirth and sweet discoursing,
Welcome and beguile his stay,
Through the summer's fervid glowing,
Through the stormy winter day.

Youth is fleeting like the blossoms;
Let not love with them depart:
Through the toils and cares of manhood
Let him soothe and cheer thy heart.

Count no gift for him too costly:
Count no toil for him too hard;
'Tis but cheap to win his blessing,
'Tis but light for his reward.

All his treasures will he give thee;
With his jewels crown thy head;
Heavenly fruit for fading blossoms,
Angel's food for earthly bread.

Fresher roses at thy portal;
Fairer clusters on thy vine;
Ampler harvests for thanksgiving:
Richer oil and sweeter wine.

Brighter sunshine in thy dwelling;
Calmer peace within thy breast;
Joy, all joys of earth excelling;
Safeguard for thy midnight rest.

Youth immortal, fadeless beauty;
Wisdom's gateway opened wide;
No more asking light for duty,
Love himself thy light and guide.

VISIT TO MY OLD HOME.

AGAIN I sought—when years had passed
Since I had left its portals last,—
That home, so dear, of childhood's pleasures,—
Its woodland paths, its hills and streams,
Whose pebbles e'en were fancied treasures,
Whose green fields, kingdoms, in its dreams.

Towards the loved home-scene eager steps
Through the green wood-path bore me on:
No welcome hoping from kind lips,
If I should cross the threshold stone,
Since all who knew me there were gone;

And, as my home, I might no more
Return within its ancient door.

The weather-beaten mansion stood
In its familiar aspect still;
But unknown faces looked abroad,
As up I came the grass-grown road,
And from the green encircling hill
Was hewn away its crest of wood.
Half-tilled, and rude and desolate,
The little garden round me lay,
And, all abandoned to their fate,
The rough stone walls were fallen away;
Unpruned, the trees ail wildly tossed
Their long decaying branches round,
And tall weeds their rank foliage crossed,
All o'er the garden ground.

I passed along; yet not less dear
The friendly scene, nor loved I less
To gaze, and muse and wander there,
Though it had grown a wilderness.

'Twas Autumn. In an Autumn hour
I last had bid the scene adieu;
But paler seemed each leaf and flower,
With the sere season's fading hue,
And more unsheltered each old bower,
Than to my childhood's view;

Smaller each rock and tree had grown—
Narrower each valley I had known;
And low and puny looked the wall,
So formidable once, and tall.
There stood the tree where I had graved
The frail memorial of my name,
Yet tottering, as though scarcely saved
From the last storm that o'er it came.
With almost every line effaced
Of the rude carving I had traced.
There stood the orchard too, with green
And Autumn's yellow fruitage crowned;
Yet traces of decay were seen
On every mossy trunk around;
And here and there a feebler one
Among their stately ranks was gone.

Embowered by leafy groves, there lay
Green path-worn hills, that circled wide
Our home, and reached the orchard side;
Those pleasant groves were hewn away—
The hills were shorn of all their pride,
And boughs in dreary heaps were strewn
Where the sweet wild flowers once had grown;
And open to the sunshine wide
The secrets of the shade were thrown.

There was no other change, save what

The tireless hand of Time had wrought,—
A hand that never learned to spare,
However dear its victims are—
That leaves no secret shrine unswept,
Which in the wildwood we have kept
Sacred to childhood's memory.
Yes—there was one more change: the soul
Of home was gone—all that had made
The garden and the woodland shade
Beloved; and that around the whole
Had thrown that spell we cannot break;
Which, to the child, doth ever make
A paradise of home—a spot
For which his love is ne'er forgot.

The kind looks and the pleasant smiles
That made perennial Summer there,
As tropic suns to Indian isles
The same warm glances ever bear—
These threw their blessed radiance o'er
The friendly scenes of home no more.
And, as the plumage of the bird
Where in the glow of sunbeams play
A thousand gorgeous hues, doth fade
Soon as the beams are turned away;
So when the smiles which once had thrown
Their happy sunshine there were gone,
One melancholy tinge came o'er

Each dear spot where so sweetly played
The bright, warm tints of love before,
And on each cloud a rainbow made,
That its calm summer heavens bore.
I had been led in distant ways,
And lovelier vales, and brighter flowers,
And greener hills and statelier bowers,
Beheld, in glow of Summer's rays,
And gentler hues of Spring's young days,
And golden mist that o'er them plays
Through the warm Indian Summer hours;
Yet none could seem so dear to me,
However beautiful or new—
However lovely they might be
In the warm Summer's glorious hue,
As home's old, gray and moss-grown bowers.
Its fields and its familiar flowers,
That once I knew and loved so well;
Where every rock and tree could tell
Stories of happy by-gone hours.

I turned me towards the ancient wood,
That still in its green grandeur stood,
Whence, in the Spring, at even-fall
The whippoorwill was wont to call,
And even to wander forth, and pour
His plaintive song before our door.
The feathery brake grew rank and tall

Within the shades, and underneath
My feet was crushed full many a wreath
Of tangled wild flowers, that had grown
And spent their odors there unknown.
The wood-path, that so oft had led
Our feet beneath the summer shade,
To the green play-haunts of our love
In the cool coverts of the grove,
Or guided to the house of prayer,
When the still Sabbath hushed the air,—
Was now untrodden, and almost
Among the bramble thickets lost.

A stillness gloomier and more deep
Than that the peaceful Sabbath gave,
Through those green places seemed to sleep,
As though above the lonely grave
Of the bright past—the joyous hours—
Life's lovely, faded vernal flowers—
The light and happy fantasies
Of that fresh morn when youth was waking
To the full sense of all that lies
In beauty's world, upon it breaking
With all the glory that may glow
Upon the mortal eye below.

With what a melancholy tone
Came on my ear the wild bird's scream!

As in those shades I stood alone,
And dreamed again the happy dream
Of childhood's days, forever gone.
Gone! 'tis the dirge of every joy;
The vain and mournful echo-note
That on the passing breeze doth float,
To mock us with its memory.

Such is the tale of life. No day
That dawns upon this mortal shore
Wears the same freshness in its ray
With which the dawn arose before.
No Spring, that with the sun returns,
With bloom and green the earth to strew,
But o'er some faded beauty mourns,
And flowers, amid sepulchral urns,
Are watered with its dew.

HEAVENLY MINISTRATIONS.

LILIAS.

SWEET Hope, that, in our weary pilgrimage,
Dost strew our way with roses; but too oft,
With thorny roses; yet we soon forget
The thorns, in tasting the perfumes they yield.

ROSA.

Yet there's a blossom sweeter yet than these,
Which wither often ere 'tis noon; but that
Grows fresher still with the declining sun,
And gladdens with enduring loveliness,
After the thousand false, deceitful flowers,
Whose gaudy glitter cheats us for a while,
Have passed away, and left no fruit behind.
It's name's Content; how happy he who finds it!

LILIAS.

Yet these two are not strangers to each other,
Content and Hope; for oftentimes they sit
Together, twining of fresh leaves and flowers,
Garlands of fadeless beauty for their heads,
Who wait in patience for the blessed gifts.
And in each other's faces, as they sit,
They look with loving smiles; and as they look,
Hope grows more trustful, and content more meek,
And more of heaven beams from her quiet eyes.

ROSA.

True, sister: they are angels which God sends,
To pour sweet balm on weary hearts, to lighten
The cares of earth, its mourners to console,
And to make earth itself as much like heaven
As mortal hearts can bear or eyes behold.

LILIAS.

Nay, God hath never left this world of sin,
Without kind angel visitors, whose hands
Were filled with blessings. He hath never sent
The weary and the sorrowing ones to walk
Through the dark pathways of affliction's twilight,
Without a heavenly guardian to stand near,
The fainting heart to strengthen, and to bring
Again, with gentlest art, the wandering thought,
To look to Him alone for every good.

ROSA.

There have been ever some who dreamed of angels
Watching o'er those whom Innocence and Love
Kept tender-hearted through life's stormy day;
But they were idle dreamers, in the view
Of a cold, faithless world, that only smiled
A careless and contemptuous smile, and turned
Its blear eyes downward on its wretched heaps
Of baubles and of perishable dust.

LILIAS.

And yet what heart so cold, so far from heaven,
But it hath sometimes felt the blessed breath
Of heavenly gales, or hath been made aware
Of influences from a higher sphere
Than that to which bleak selfishness confines
The narrowed soul? Hath not the vernal soil,
At least of childhood, with those dews been wet,

Which fall in angel-watches, and which nourish
Sweet flowers, that make us happier, till the night
Of Autumn scatters all the earth with frost?

ROSA.

How soon the heat exhales the early dew,
When Summer's sun rides high! How fast the chains
Of earth and sense lock up the willing heart
In walls of adamant, and make the ear
Too heavy to be charmed by angel songs—
The eye too dim to look beyond the clouds
That curtain round the porticoes of time!
And heaven itself seems only as a dream
Of those whom bitter disappointment fills
With discontent of earth.

LILIAS.

Yet Heaven forsakes not
The hearts that close themselves against its love,
But with kind ministrations ever seeks
To win the lost and wandering back to life.
And if the honey-cells of earthly flowers,
It fills with heavenly nectar, are passed by
With stolid carelessness, or worse than this,
Are turned to bitter venom, by the craft
Of sensual malice,—does it shut its hand,
And leave its rebel children to be starved
By the vile tares they plant, and call them bread?
Does it not rather lavish out new gifts,

And labor with new art to ope the eyes
So blind to every blessing, and to wake
Dead hearts to feel the warming glow of Spring?

Let us be thankful that so dear a faith
Is now set forth as in the light of day;
That the fond hopes, the dim presentiments,
The inward longings, which the single-hearted
Of darker ages cherished, are fulfilled;
And the uncertain light to which they clung,
As mariners for guidance to pale stars,
That glimmer through the rifts of murky clouds,
Has brightened into sunshine glad and clear.

THE LIGHT OF LIFE.

O LIGHT of joy! O blessed light!
That cheers the good man's path, and makes
Earth's lowliest, darkest valleys bright
With heavenly splendor where it breaks!
What heartfelt peace, what fearless trust
Are his, who, guided by its ray,
Unfalteringly, treads the narrow way,
And finds the blessing of the just,

The shining of a perfect day.
Though tempests compass him around,
And spend their lightnings o'er his head,
The almighty arms his steps surround,
And safely through the storm he's led.
And then he sees the promise-bow
Spanning the heavens,—the holy sign
Of mercy, peace and love divine,
Dwelling with man below.

There will be hours in each one's life,
When gloomy thoughts come crowding on,
Like phalanxes to martial strife,—
Like clouds before the morning sun;
When from each dear thing of our love,
The bright enchantment fades away;
And then, to him who hath above
No treasured hope of brighter day,
How sadly o'er his gilded sky,
Comes the cold storm-cloud, to destroy
The fleeting summer of his joy!

'Tis not for nought that God hath made
A curtain-cloud at times to fall
Upon that heart, with withering shade,
That seeks not in his love its all.
'Tis that there is no other home
But under his protecting hand—

That those who from his care would roam
Godless, to seek a dwelling land,
Deceive themselves; to teach this truth
He sets before our eyes the cloud
That hides the cherished hopes of youth,
The darkness and the veil that shroud
Our loveliest prospects, and make dim
Each star-lamp of our life, that ever
Receiveth not its light from Him.
Thus would He lead us to enjoy
That light which knows no fading—love
Which grows not cold, without alloy,
Which comes alone from Him above.

But still we trim our taper blaze,
And cherish its expiring light,
Unmindful of the immortal rays
That make the mountain-summits bright,
Nor dream that our own shadows throw
The darkness and the chill of night
Across the murky vales below,
While the eternal sunbeams glow
Undimmed upon the mount of God,
The light of heaven, a quenchless flood,
Wrath to the faithless, blessing to the good.

HEAVENLY WELCOME.

'MID the bell's funereal tolling,
'Mid the weeping of the mourners,
In the stillness of the chamber
Where the white-robed dead was laid,—
Seemed to sound a joyful anthem,
Seemed to echo the dear welcome
Of another risen angel,
Passed to light from earth's dark shade.

One more gone to join the number
Of the host of the redeemed ones,
Who from glad thanksgiving cease not,
Singing His Almighty love,
Who had bought them, who had brought them
To His house of many mansions,
Children of the Marriage Supper
Of the Lamb of God, above.

One more freed from earthly sorrows,
Earthly trials and temptations,
Passed the gates of death forever,
Welcomed to an angel's home.
In the midst of all the mourning,
In the sad funereal stillness,
Through the din of worldly tumult,
Seemed the blissful peal to come,

Of the anthem of her greeting,
Almost caught by mortal hearing,
As a sweet-voiced chorus, blending
With a lofty organ strain.
We have lost, but heaven has won her;
Be consoled, ye friends that mourn her,
Lost but for a little season;
Hers is everlasting gain.

ON THE RIGHT HAND.

"COME YE BLESSED OF MY FATHER."

COME, from beds of painful sickness;
Come, from dark and sorrowful dwellings:
Come, from fiery fields of battle;

Come, inherit heaven at last!
Ye who have on earth been faithful
Servants of your Lord and Master,
Come, your days of strife are past.

Come, ye mourners over loved ones
Passed the gates of death before you,
Friendless, fatherless and widows,
Lone and weary, sick and sad;
He hath tried your souls as silver;
From the dross of sin hath purged you;
In His house shall make you glad.

Lovers, by strange fortune driven
Far from hope and from each other,
Daily seeking consolation
In His love that faileth not;
Come, where seas no more shall part you,
Finding more than ye have prayed for:
All your tears be now forgot.

Ye who labored cheerless, hopeless,
Through oppression and misfortune,
Poor, uncared for and unpitied;—
Rich alone in faith and love;
Come, your earthly toils are ended.
Come, ye blessed of your Father,
There is joy for you above.

All whom darkly, but in mercy,
He hath led through vales of sorrow,
Through temptations great and fearful,—
  Come, your warfare now is o'er.
He whose word of truth has kept you,
Whom ye have not vainly trusted,
  Gives you peace forevermore.

Ye who thirst for living waters,
Hunger for the bread of heaven,
Pure in heart and poor in spirit,
  Come, and find in God your rest!
He shall lead you, He shall feed you
With eternal consolations;
  With His love and likeness blest.

VIOLET-BUDS.

A THOUSAND violet buds lie sleeping
  Beneath the withered blades of grass:
And wintry winds, above them sweeping,
  Make mournful music as they pass.

The drifting snows of bleak December
  Fall thick and heavy where they rest;

While we, as in a dream, remember
  The fields in green and beauty dressed.

Spring shall awake the slumbering blossoms
  To greet the sunny skies of May;
While laughing children deck their bosoms
  With violet-wreaths in happy play.

Beneath the snows of age are lying
  Fresh violet buds of love and hope,
For sun and breath of spring time sighing
  To call their purple blossoms up.

Alas! no earthly spring shall ever
  Awake these Autumn buds to bloom;
The evening sun's pale beams can never
  Thaw the cold ground, so near the tomb.

The sunshine of a heavenly morrow
  Shall call their beauty forth to view;
And their unshadowed leaves shall borrow
  A purer sky's immortal blue.

No bud so deep, so darkly buried,
  But love's warm beams shall find their way
To the cold prison where it tarried,
  And welcome it to heavenly day.

HOPE.

THE voice of Hope is ever singing:
Silvery voiced Hope!
Her sweet, clear notes are ever ringing,
To cheer the drinkers of affliction's cup.
To the weary she is bringing
Blossoms fresh from Eden's bowers;
The harp of gladness newly stringing,
She bids its music soothe our twilight hours.
Who, oh who shall say
That all her dear enchantments are delusion?
Who bid us cast away
Her garlands, gathered from the rich profusion
Of bloom that opens in celestial day?
O welcome, angel Hope! thy blossoms linger
Late on the Autumn field of sadness;
Doth not God send thee to us, thou sweet singer
Of joy and gladness?
Doth He not send thee hither,

With promises of blessings kept in store
For those who, through misfortune's wintry weather,
With patient and with trustful heart endure?
For not to a rewardless strife
Doth Heaven invite us; all sincere the call
To overcome and share eternal life.
Thy banner, Hope, for all
To gather courage from, is wide outspread
In sunlight, as the rainbow, to adorn
And cheer life's lowering battle-morn,
Even o'er the lowliest, weariest toiler's head.
O happy they who, as they look, behold
Above the banner starred with gold,
Faith with her sister Hope join hands, and hear
Her words of heavenly cheer;
And learn of her to tread
With firmer step the upward ways that lead
To blissful dwellings, and with manlier heart,
Of this life's toils and woes to bear their part.
And they shall win the field,
And bear away the victor's palm, and know
What living vigor Virtue's laurels yield,--
What cordial fruits are those which grow
Upon the trees that stand
Beside the paths, on either hand,
Which lead the worthy and the wise
Into her Paradise,
In the Immortal Land.

SONG OF THE RED LILY.

I AM the red field lily; the sky
Of summer bends o'er me with deep blue eye;
The butterfly flutters above my breast,
And the ground-bird hides by my side her nest.

I come when the early flowers are gone,
That the Spring delighted to look upon;
And with gayer and statelier ones than before
The meadows are gilded and purpled o'er;
But I stand in glory above them all,
With Summer's crimson coronal.

Sweet odors from many a flower are borne
On the wakeful gale of the dewy morn;
The lonely orchis, in forest shade,
In pictured mantle may be arrayed;
But alone, in my gorgeous vesture, I rise,
And unfold my heart to the summer skies.

Ask ye, who painted my cup so bright,
With the richest hues of the noon-day light?
What fingers fashioned my graceful stem
To bear up its ruby diadem?
What skill, surpassing all human power,
My delicate tissues of leaf and flower,
Has woven with beauty so rich and rare,
With robes of monarchs beyond compare?

'Tis He, ye know, who maketh for all,
His sun to shine and his rain to fall;
Who feeds the sparrow, and hears the cry
Of the humblest creature beneath the sky;
And will not He, surely, who has such care
For the flowers of the field and the birds of the air,
Much more his mercy and kindness show,
O faithless children of men, to you?

FOR A CLERGYMAN'S ALBUM.

IN sorrow and affliction,
The messenger of peace
Must toil to make the tender plants
Of good and truth increase.

The banner of the Gospel
Must float o'er fortress-towers,
And Christian men must soldiers be
Against infernal powers.

Six days of toil and and battle
Their bravest strength demand,
Before they find their Sabbath rest
Upon the promised land.

Be strong then, and have courage,
Thou that art called to stand
A watchman on the city walls,
With weapons in thine hand.

Though foes without and foes within
The heritage assail,
The Word of truth shall over all
In victory prevail.

THE MORNING STAR.

SERENELY beautiful, the morning star
Shone through my window and proclaimed the day,
It shone upon my pillow as I lay.
Morn after morn I saw and watched it there:

And thought how quietly it had looked down
On all the tumult and the strife of earth,
Through the long ages since creation's birth,
Nor lost one jewel from its radiant crown.

And then of that blest star I thought, whose ray
Guided the Eastern Magi to the place
Where humbly lay the Lord of life and grace,
Born as an infant into earthly day.

But now, He dwells in mortal flesh no more;
The "man of sorrows" now is glorified;
And Him, whom earth a resting place denied,
As King and Lord, the heavens of heavens adore.

He is their sun; they see His glory there,
Unclouded and undimmed, while we below
See one bright beam of the celestial glow
Shining upon us, as the morning star.

Arise, O heavenly Morning Star, and shine
Within my heart, so cold and dark and dead;
And teach my soul, whatever way I tread,
That all the light and all the life is Thine.

THE SEED OF KNOWLEDGE.

O PRECIOUS seed, in by-gone times so rare!
Only by sages gathered up with pain,
Now scattered wide for every soul to share,
Like the o'erflowing blessing of the rain,
That waters every hill and every plain.

O precious seed! how carelessly unsought
By the short-sighted children of to-day!
With what rich blessings is the morrow fraught,
For those who wake to gather them; but they
Slumber the golden morning hours away.

Seed by the way-side scattered and down trod!
What bounteous fields of harvest might have crowned
The labors of a faithful hand, when God
Gave dew and sunshine to the waiting ground!
How fruitless is the idle summer found!

Heaven's daily blessings seem too cheap to prize;
The constant light, that with its golden shower,
Illumes and blesses our unthinking eyes,
And the sweet air that fans us hour by hour,
And feeds the thankless breast with vital power.

So truth shines out with such unstinted light,
Our hearts grow senseless of its power and worth;—
And we forget how sad and dark a night
Time past, was brooding o'er the slumbering earth,
Ere knowledge's clear water-brooks sprang forth.

Yet not in vain the sunshine and the dew,—
The seed in many a furrow cast abroad;
Even now, earth blossoms to angelic view;
And fields the wise with patient toil have trod,
Shall yield rich harvests in the sight of God.

HOPE AND SPRING.

SPRING and Hope are sisters dear;
Ever walk they hand in hand;
When the sky is blue and clear,
Go they singing through the land,

Weaving of new leaves and flowers,
Garlands for the naked bowers.

Spring and Hope together come;
With the May-day sun they smile,
In glad hearts they make their home;
And the sower's toil beguile,
With the promise of ripe grain,
When the Autumn comes again.

Ever welcome guests are they,
Whether at the palace gate,
Or the the cot beside the way,
With their precious gifts they wait;
Making every bosom glad,
That the winter storms made sad.

Wide is opened every door,—
Every heart to Hope and Spring.
Prince and peasant, rich and poor,
Share alike the gifts they bring.
Happy-hearted children play,
Strewing blossoms in their way.

O that Charity might be
Such a welcome guest with men!
Every portal opened free
To receive the angel in.
Discontent and want and woe
Homes and hearts no more should know.

"TIME IS MONEY."

SO says the worldling, who, with downcast eye,
Intent upon his shining heaps of gold,
Counts no day fortunate that does not add
Wealth to his coffers. Thus he coins his time
To gold; and heavily the passing hours
Drop petrified to lifeless ore beneath
His hands, and downward, like the magnet, draw
His beggar heart, which daily seems to grow
More earthly, and more like the dross he loves.
What can his treasures purchase? Honor, fame,
Preferment, ease or pleasure? The next breath
Of air may waft them like thin smoke away.
Love, friendship, happiness and peace of heart?
Nay, these are all too far beyond the reach
Of this poor world to give,—how poor to him
Who asks for lasting blessings at its hand!

But what is time to him, who, while he walks
The earth, still breathes the air of heaven, and sees
Beyond earth's shadowy vale, the immortal fields?
A passing moment, but of priceless worth!
A fleeting day, in which to do the work
For which eternity can find no room—
Which all eternity can ne'er undo!
A day of Spring in which to sow the seed,
Of which the next world the ripe harvest gives.
Treasures hath time more rich than gold or gems;
Seize them to-day, or they are lost forever.
Thou hast no warrant of to-morrow's gifts.
To-day alone is thine, and thou art made
A steward in it, to give good account
Of what thou doest, when its sun is set,
And the night comes, "in which no man can work."

THE FOREST TEMPLE.

THE wood-path seemed a porch
To one of Nature's temples, wide and high,
Where underneath the forest's living arch,
Bright blossom-pavements lie.

Green, blooming shrubs around
Threw incense of rich odors on the air,
Close walling in the temple's holy ground
With beauty rich and rare.

Amid the fragrant bloom,
The ripe blue clusters of the bilberry hung,
While high amid the maple's shadowy gloom
The clinging wild vine swung.

There, through the leafy aisles,
A rapturous anthem each fresh dawn awakes,
That like heaven's music, with day's earliest smiles,
The hallowed stillness breaks.

And softer, when the breeze
Of quiet evening through the red sky floats,
The feathered singers, from the dusky trees,
Send up their vesper notes.

For Nature's choristers,
In the wood temples, are the singing birds,
Whose guileless hymn as pure devotion stirs,
As solemn chanted words.

Methinks the red man there
To the Great Spirit bowed in solemn awe,
And offered silently his simple prayer,
And joyous omens saw,

In passing of wild birds,
In playing of soft lights among the trees,
Or deemed he heard the Spirit's answering words,
In murmurs of the breeze.

O Thou, before whose sight
The holiest temple is the obedient heart,
Who in proud marble fanes hast no delight,
This grace, we pray, impart:

That we may ever hear,
Where'er we go, thy footsteps and thy voice,
Making the solitude and desert drear
To blossom and rejoice.

THE FLOWER GARDEN.

THERE are blossoms in thy garden,
Every summer blooming fair;
But that they may grow and flourish,
They demand thy constant care.

With the first spring bud's unfolding
  Must thy cares and toils begin;
Not to cease till Autumn's latest
  Blossoms all are gathered in.

But I know of flowers more lovely
  Than the fairest ones which grow,
Soon to die, in earthly gardens:
  Bright immortal flowers I know.

Flowers of Goodness, Truth and Virtue;
  Plant them in thy choicest ground;
In the garden of thy spirit
  Let no baneful weed be found.

Labor for these tender nurslings
  Of a heavenly soil and clime.
They demand more watchful culture
  Than the plants of earth and time.

All thy spring-time, all the summer
  Of thy life, they ask thy guard.
In thy ripe and golden Autumn,
  They will give their rich reward.

They will give their hallowed sweetness,
  When thy earthly joys are fled;
Clustering in immortal garlands
  Round the Christian's dying bed.

THE CHRISTIAN'S GARDEN.

THE Christian man hath a garden
  Of beauty wondrous and rare;
There are bright and fragrant blossoms,
  And fruit-trees green and fair.

There is Love with her fadeless roses,
  And Faith, that each morn looks up
The rising sun to welcome,
  With her fresh and dewy cup.

There is Truth, pure, white and spotless,
  And Hope, that with open eye
Looks upward through storm and winter,
  Cheerfully, trustfully.

There is Charity, ever radiant
  With Summer's sunny glow,
And Mercy, sweet flower of heaven,
  Blossoming here below.

There is Patience, that long endureth,
  And Pity, with pearly tear,
While Joy crowns with smiling garlands
  Each season of the year.

The Lord, the heavenly Sower,
  Hath planted this garden fair,
And His love still watches o'er it,
  With tender and constant care.

The sun of heaven doth cherish
  With its kindly heat and light,
Each tree of the Father's planting,
  Each blossom of beauty bright.

The Vine hangs with purple clusters,
  The Fig tree its sweetness gives,
The Olive with green and fatness
  On every hill-top thrives.

There is fruit for the soul that hungers,
  And longs to be daily fed
With manna, like the angels,
  With true and living bread.

The Lord such a garden giveth
  To his servants to keep and till,
That they therein may labor
  Daily to do his will.

He planteth, but they must water;
  A servant's part is theirs,
Faithful to guard and keep it,
  If they would hereafter be heirs.

THE NEW JERUSALEM.

BEHOLD the heavenly city stand,
  High on a mount, in noonday light,
With blessings filled from God's right hand,
Walled in with jasper, clear and bright.

Wide open stand its pearly gates,
Inviting all to enter in,
To tread with joy its golden streets,
And wisdom's starry crown to win.

There flows the eternal river, clear
As crystal from the throne of God;
There trees with healing leaves appear,
And heavenly fruits for angel's food.

But who are they whose happy feet
On Zion's hill shall stand secure?
They in whose mouths is no deceit;
Whose hands are clean, whose hearts are pure.

These are the blessed who shall be
Like fruitful trees by living streams;
And such shall dwell, O Lord, with thee,
Where thy eternal sunlight beams.

THE MOURNER'S HOPE.

IF it were now instead of long ago,
For the first time proclaimed, that those who die
Shall rise again to immortality,—
If, like an unexpected morning glow
Breaking the darkness of a hopeless night,
The joyful news of life beyond the tomb,
Brought by some heavenly messenger, had come,—
How soon might Sorrow's downcast eye grow bright,
The heavy heart grow light,
That mourned for dear and lost ones, as the day
Drives the cold twilight shadows far away.

And is it now so long
Since the glad promise woke the ear of Faith,
Of better life beyond the gates of death,
That like an old, almost forgotten song,
It cheers no longer? for we mourn as though
Our faith itself were dead,
As though dear hopes had fled,
And left our souls to vain regret and woe.

You say, Our eyes are dim;
We cannot see so far.
Gone,—and we know not where!
We can but weep for him!

Mourn then; but let your grief
Be tempered with belief
In what we cannot see with mortal eyes;
Trust in the tender love
Of Him who rules above,
All-merciful, Almighty, and All-wise;
With faith in him who gave
His life our lives to save,
Who calls the sleeping dead, and they arise,
And brings his children home
Through the gateway of the tomb
Into the gladness of his Paradise.

BUDS.

BUDS to garland infant foreheads,
Crimson leaf-tips peeping through!
New blown roses, fair and fragrant,
In the path of childhood strew!
Blushing roses, brightly jeweled
With the freshest morning dew.

Ah, how soon the fires of passion
  Wither up the youthful bloom!
Ah, how oft the sunny morning
  Changes to a night of gloom!
And the lovely head of beauty
  Sinks to an unworthy tomb.

Plant ye deep in spring-time furrows
  Love's and truth's immortal seed.
Give ye, through the weary Summer,
  Rain of tears and patient heed!
So in Autumn ye may gather
  Ripe and blessed fruit indeed.

THE LEAVES AND THE BLOSSOMS.

SUGGESTED BY ONE OF RICHTER'S GERMAN "PARABLES."

JOYOUSLY the light of May was glowing
On the fresh and tender budding foliage,
Bathing all the forest in the glory
Of the Spring's delightful, rosy morning.
With the apple blooms the winds were playing,
Shaking to the ground a fragrant shower
Now and then, that whitened all the greensward.
By the blooming orchard passed the poet;
And it seemed to him the wanton zephyrs

Laughed to see the mimic snow-storm blowing
From the apple trees; and as he listened,
With his bosom full of spring-time gladness,
Thus, so seemed it, to the falling blossoms,
Spake the firm green leaves with exultation:

Ye vain and gaudy blossoms,
How quick ye fade away!
While we grow greener, brighter still
Through all the summer day.

And when the frosted Autumn
Her spell around us throws,
Long after ye have passed away—
How bright our vesture glows!

Thus spake the leaves in Spring-time;
And thus replied the flowers:
We wish not to remain, and deck
With you the summer bowers;

For we have gifts more precious
On Autumn to bestow,
Than all the purple and the gold
Of your decaying show.

Hidden within our bosoms
The costly fruit is born;
So, though we perish quick away,
O treat us not with scorn!

For ye shall shortly wither
  Before the Autumnal blast,
And on the forest's frosted floor
  In ruined heaps be cast:

And they who pluck our fruits, shall tread
  Your scattered ruins o'er,
And while they bless God for the flowers,
  Shall think of you no more.

CONSOLATION.

I KNOW the darkness will not always last;
  That soon or late will glow the crimson dawn:
Earth shall not be forever frozen fast,
  And Winter's snow will by and by be gone.

I know that howsoever angrily
  The storm may rage, a calm will some time come;
And the worn mariner, weary of the sea,
  Shall reach at length his haven and his home.

And so I trust, and feel myself assured,
  The woes and sorrows which oppress to-day,
However long and heavily endured,
  Shall by and by grow light and pass away.

I know our loving Father cannot mean
  That we should suffer with no good in view.
What though the good be far off and unseen?
  The Lord hath promised it: his word is true.

He that hath smitten us will bind us up:
  Will feed the souls that hunger for his bread;
Will fill for us the emptied bitter cup
  With heavenly wine; anoint the downcast head

With oil of joy for mourning. He will give
  Beauty for ashes, songs of praise for sorrow;
And raise us from the dead, that we may live
  And bless His name, in heaven's eternal morrow.

LEARNING AND LIFE.

Read at a reunion of the former pupils of the Mount Pleasant Classical Institution, at Amherst, August, 1847, fifteen years after the closing of the school.

WHEN towards the coming years we turn our eyes,
  In youth's fresh morning, brightly stretches out,
Beyond our farthest view, a blooming path,
Inviting us to tread its hopeful way.
But when the road is travelled, and the gay
Illusions have passed by, how short, how vain,
Appear the hasty years! what few results

Of solid and enduring good remain!
And over time misspent we sigh, and say,
Alas, the vanity of human life!

We grow not wise at once. As far below
Its real worth, our disappointed hearts
View the lamented past, as we before
Had overrated its prospective good.
But would'st thou learn how little to expect
From the short-sighted labors of a day,—
Look up—behold the orbs of heaven, that wheel
With tireless flight in wondrous circles round.
And, if thy intellect can bear the task,
Labor to comprehend the mighty plan:
And then look back upon our little globe,
Whose years are but as moments, when compared
With stellar orbits—whose wide spreading fields,
And wider oceans, are as viewless specks
In the broad regions of celestial space.

But yet another prospect must be scanned,
Ere we have learned to weigh in equal scales
At once the greatness and the littleness
Of human nature and of human life.
If thou the value of thy life compute
Alone by what to-day appears, thou must
Misjudge it. 'Tis but seed-time with thee now—
At most, the springing of the summer blade:

Thy harvest an eternal morrow is.
Wondrous as that bright alphabet of stars
Appears, in which our nothingness we read,
Its glory fades to night, its gold is dust,
Viewed from the world on which that morrow breaks:
And yet the glory of that world is thine;
And we shall wake and find ourselves a part
Of that immortal universe, whose cycles
Time hath no measure to compute, nor space
A line its boundaries to circumscribe.

Thus with a double aspect doth our life
Appear in Wisdom's eye; and thus doth He
Who made us, first with prodigies of power
O'erwhelm us in humility, that He
May safely afterwards make known how great
The blessing that awaits the humble heart.

Our years of studentship, we say, are past;
But we are learners still. The world itself
Is but a school, where every day are set
Before our eyes new lessons to be learned,
New tasks appointed for our hands to try.
We all are teachers too; and, well or ill,
We give out lessons which our neighbors learn.
Each silent deed with eloquent tongue persuades;
Example preaches oft with more success
Than all who stand in pulpits, and proclaim

Truths little practised, and—perchance—forgot
By priest and hearer both, by Sabbath eve.
We may grow wiser daily, if we will:
We may stand fools upon the very top
Of Science's hill; and die like those who starve,
Laden with gold and gems, in desert lands.

The skill to learn, the wisdom well to use,
Not always meet. The wisest ones are oft
The most profoundly ignorant of what
The world calls wisdom, and of that for which
The schools grant honors, titles and degrees.
Then let us hear, as down the rapid stream
Of Time, we float, the sweet but earnest song
The angel of our life sings as we go,
While pointing to the landmarks on our way,
Warning us that amid the varied charms
Which Nature, Learning, Science, Truth, afford,
We seek our wisdom in this noblest truth,
That without love to Him who gives them all,
And love to man our brother, all is vain
That we have learned, or done, or yet shall do.

THE OLD ORCHARD.

TREES whose green and blossom
  Cheered my childhood's eye;
In whose cooling shadows,
  When the sun was high,
Playful toil beguiled me
  Through the summer hours,
Once again I greet you,
  Old and friendly bowers.

Here the sweetest music
  Of the matin bird,
At the early coming
  Of the spring was heard;
Here the loveliest blossoms
  Field or forest knew,
Bathed their tender leaflets
  In the summer dew.

And the yellow autumn
  Here before us spread

Her delicious treasures,
  As, with rustling tread,
Came she by with garlands
  Of the vine and sheaf,
And entwined her tresses
  With the last green leaf:

Though a tone of sadness
  All our joy came o'er,
As red leaves were mingled
  With the golden store;
And the frosty winter
  Followed in her train,
And his snow-flakes scattered
  Where her fruits had lain.

Venerable orchard!
  Verse delights to tell,
In thy green recesses
  What sweet memories dwell;
Like the birds, that fondly
  To thy cool retreat
Cling for kindly shelter
  From the summer heat.

O how many like us,
  Thy green shades beneath,

Have of Hope's gay blossoms
  Twined the smiling wreath,
And delighted hung it
  On some friendly bough,
But to see it shattered
  By the storm, ere now!

Be it so; all scattered
  Childhood's gathered flowers;
Leafless, torn, uprooted,
  All its greenest bowers;
Nay, its friends departed,
  Dearest, kindest, best,
In whose happy presence
  Our young hearts were blest.

Grieve not at their passing;
  Look not wistful back
From thy manhood's prospects,
  To the narrow track,
Worn by childish footsteps:
  Idly shalt thou there
Shrines of joys departed
  Labor to repair.

Pleasures glow and vanish
  As the seasons wane;

Joys, earth-born, like flowers,
  Earthward turn again:
Think not to retain them
  With a miser's hand:
All their gold shall moulder
  In thy grasp to sand.

Yet know well, one sunbeam
  Ne'er is taken away
From the glowing noontide
  Of thy summer day,
But to gild the morrow
  With a happier light:
Rest then, calm and trustful
  Through the stormy night.

MY INHERITANCE.

A SCANTY bit of barren soil,
  Profuse alone of useless weeds,
Is all the ground where I must toil,
To plant and gather heavenly seeds.
God grant me, hoping, not in vain,
His blessed sunshine and his rain.

God grant me strength and patience still,
To labor in my narrow field.
With patient doing of His will,
The poorest ground some fruit may yield.
And one ripe grain of wheat is more
To Him than Sodom's wealthiest store.

Shall I my single talent hide,
And leave my heritage to waste,
Because it is not rich and wide,
And under tropic sunshine placed?
And when my Lord his tithes shall claim,
How can I bear the idler's shame?

No, let me not complain how small
My portion, but how little good
My weariest summer's work could call
Out of the ground I ploughed and hoed.
Alas! with barrenness and drought,
And frost, I almost vainly fought.

I dream of gardens broad and fair,
With many a lovely blossom sown.
A few frail plants exhaust my care;
The rest is all with weeds o'ergrown.
Farewell, vain dreams! It now remains
To cull my few ripe harvest grains.

How scant the store! yet strange to tell,
My board is still with bounty spread.
Always, by some kind miracle,
Are multiplied my loaves of bread;
My homely water turned to wine.
Thanks for the blessing, all divine!

TRUE LIFE.

THE more thou puttest in the Lord thy trust,
  The stronger shall thine arm for service be:
When thou rememberest that thou art but dust,
  Then first awakes a living soul in thee.

When thou canst say, O Lord, thy will be done,
  Then shall *thy* arm grow strong for truth and right;
When thou despairest, thou hast first begun
  To learn from whence the feeble heart hath might.

When thou hast gained a victory o'er a foe,
  Hast prayed in fear for storms to break away,
Then first the peace of angels shalt thou know,
  Shalt feel how sweet is heaven's unclouded day.

When thou with cheerful zeal for virtue's part,
  Enchanting Pleasure's rose-path shall forsake,
Then first true joy shall warm and bless thy heart,
  And heavenly blossoms by thy side awake.

When with unfaltering courage thou hast sought
On duty's battle-field thy prize to win,
And, in thy self-forgetfulness, hast thought
The world too little to be gained by sin,

Then hast thou first grown master of thyself—
Thy meaner self hast conquered; and shalt find
That thou hast well disdained the slavish pelf.
Of the base kingdom thou hast left behind.

THE WORSHIP OF LIFE.

I SAW a way ascending, where bright hills
Serene and beautiful, lay far above
The snowy mountain-tops of earth, that pierced
The cloudless ether. Thither went I up,
Till on the summit of the hills I stood,
In their pure atmosphere, as on the pavement
Of the great temple of the universe,
Of whose sublime and thousand-pillared dome,
The azure canopy that curtains earth
Is but a single arch. As there I stood,
A strain of melody entranced my ears,
Like a deep organ-peal of lofty tone,
Whose bass was as the rolling thunder's voice,

Yet calm as mighty, and serene as deep:
Filled up with sweet and wondrous harmonies.
As though the voices of all ocean's waves,
Were joined with all the voices which the wind
Brings from each mighty thing that bears its blast
With giant firmness, and each fragile thing
That bends before its gentlest whisperings.
With such profound solemnity that psalm
Its mighty and o'erpowering cadence swelled,
Yet with such gentleness and sweetness filled.
Inspiring calmest peace and heavenly trust,
I could but kneel in adoration deep;
And though I saw no living creature near,
I felt as though the universe of life
Were present, joined with me in worship there.
Surely, thought I, some seraph choir is near
Who celebrate their Sabbath here unseen.

As thus I listened, on my vision came,
As in a living picture, earth's fair fields,
Subdued to man's dominion, and replete
With all the activity of busy life.
There all the elements of nature toiled
Ceaseless for man, his tributaries all,
To drive his wheels, his spindles and his looms.
To forge his shafts, and over sea and land
His burdens and his messages to bear.

There issued forth the ploughman with his plough.
That cleft with heavy sound the fertile sod;
Down at the mower's feet the whistling scythe
Laid low the blooming burden of the field,
While creaking wains conveyed the treasure home.
There rose the vintage shout and harvest song;
Nor wanting was the lowing of the herd,
And bleat of flocks, and each sweet rural sound.
In forest deep the woodman's hearty stroke
Loud echoed; while the quarry and the mine
With din of labor sent their treasures forth.
The smith incessantly his anvil beat,
While saws and hammers with tumultuous strife
Resounded, as the builders labored on
To rear up cities, where the pulse of life
Beats more intensely, and the willing hand
Find largest scope to scatter blessings round.
There to the wave of living sound were joined
The carol of the boatman at his oar,
And sailor's shout, as with his brawny arm
He lifts the anchor, and unfurls the sail,
That speeds the wealth of nations o'er the breast
Of ocean, gathered from remotest shores.
All these with every sound of human joy
And hope, and every tone that nature breathes
From her sweet instruments, together rose
To swell that anthem of sublimest praise.

All in one harmony can Love combine,
  Because one blessing is within them all;
And their rude jar to melody refine,
  As it ascends on angel's ears to fall.

Man hears indeed but discord, when his heart
  Is closed by selfish passions to the flow
Of those pure influences which impart
  To all his being warm affection's glow;

But when he opens the soul's inner doors,
  Heaven breathes upon him, and attunes his ear,
To hear the harmonies which love restores,
  As from their homes of peace the angels hear:

The mere material sound forgotten quite,
  In presence of that spirit which displays
This truth before him in celestial light,—
  Use to the neighbor is God's highest praise.

Love in its bosom doth all blessings bear;
  Worship without it is a lifeless thing;
The breath of charity alone is prayer,
  Lifting the soul from earth on hallowed wing.

As from this high communion man descends,
  And to perform his daily duty goes,
Still with his inner thoughts that chorus blends,
  Which on his spirit's ear so sweetly rose.

The brotherhood of labor he esteems
  No servile bondage, which he fain would break,
But rather like a golden chain it seems,
  To bind all hearts in concord, and to make

All hands subservient to one common cause,
  With heaven co-workers, in a lower sphere:
Yet guided by the same eternal laws,
  That heaven may have its earthly pattern here.

THE MIRACLE OF SPRING.

ONCE more the glorious miracle is done,
And all the naked winter woods stand forth
In robes of tender green, and all the fields
Flourish with herbage and rejoice in bloom.
How great the miracle, if ne'er but once
In all the ages, Spring had garnished earth
With such magnificence of beauty, spread
So lavishly abroad in all her realm!
How happy should we deem the eyes of those
Who lived to see the glory in their day!
And is it less a miracle, that now
We see it every year renewed before us?
And is it less divine, because it grows

A thing so common, that unthinking hearts
Cease to admire the beauty, and forget,
Or never learn, that He whose Word of power
At first created earth and called it good,
Daily creates and blesses it anew.

A VISION OF HOPE.

BEYOND the deep, black river, which vessel has never passed,
High over the rock-ribbed mountains, which the strength of the Lord sets fast,
I see a beautiful country, with youth and love aglow,
Where comes no cold nor winter; where gathers no frost nor snow.

And they that have gone before us, a host that no tongue can count,
Stand in white robes and beckon to us from the shining mount.
They bid us be brave and faithful, could we but their voices hear;
They bid us endure with patience, till the day of release draws near.

Kind friends, dear brothers and sisters, sweet hope expects to meet,

Among the ransomed millions, that dwell on the golden street:
Friends for and with whom I may labor, with service however small,
So we may be brought still nearer the Lord, who does good to all.

And one who is more than sister, one who is more than friend,
Waits there to bid me welcome, her life with my own to blend;
With helpful hands for each other a paradise to make;
With joyful hearts for each other the burden of love to take.

An end to the restless warfare, an end to the painful strife,
An end to the jarring discords, that weary this earthly life:
And the trees that so many summers bloomed fruitless, shall yield their full;
And the hearts that were sad and broken, shall be glad again, and whole.

LOVE.

HOW sweet the charm where Love unites
Two kindred souls, to make
A heaven of their terrestial home,
And all the kindly graces come,
Their blessings to partake.

There Friendship finds a welcome seat,
 And Charity's a guest,
And every day of all the year
Brings peace, contentment and good cheer,
 With angels at the feast.

PROGRESS.

YOUNG Progress, once upon a time,
 Desired to take the reins,
And drive the steeds of Time himself
 Across the Western plains.

The team was safe in Steady's hands,
 But then he drove *so* slow!
Pray, father, let me try for once,—
 I'm old enough, I know.

"My son," said Steady, "You shall hear
 The counsels of your sire;
But if, well warned, you still insist,
 I grant you your desire.

"The way that we must go," said he,
 "Hath dangers not a few;
And not a single step of it
 Is known to me or you."

But Progress was a headstrong youth,
  And gave but little thought
To lessons from the lips of age,
  Howe'er with wisdom fraught.

He took the reins, on dashed the steeds;
  The way seemed smooth and plain;
The crowds, exulting, shout "Hurrah!"
  Beside the rattling wain.

What brave advances we have made,
  Is his exulting cry.
What of the rude and sluggish past
  With modern times can vie!

Down with the fences! bridge the streams!
  We'll take a shorter way;
A good time's coming, we've been told;
  We'll have it here to-day!

The glittering of the distant hills
  His eager eye engaged;
He heeded not the slippery rocks,—
  The floods that round them raged.

Too late, he saw the danger near;
  He sought escape too late!
The good time soonest comes for those
  Who bide their time and wait.

THE CHILD AND THE SEASONS.

WHAT dost thou bring for me? what dost thou bring?
Haste with thy gifts of joy, beautiful Spring.

May-flowers I bring thee, all blushing and sweet;
Violets I scatter all under thy feet;
Wind-flowers in green budding thickets I strew;
Buttercups golden I spread in your view.
Gather them quickly; enjoy them to-day;
For soon, on the morrow, they'll wither away.

What dost thou bring for me? Haste, and come near,
Beautiful Summer, so sunny and clear!

Roses I bring thee, the sweetest of June,—
Perishing roses: Oh! gather them soon.
Lilies I bring thee, that ope with the day;
But ere the sun set, they wither away.
Bright days, with golden winged sunbeams, I bring,
When the green fields laugh, and happy birds sing.
Haste to enjoy them, while bright are the hours,
Warm are the sunbeams and fresh are the flowers;

Haste, and with blessed deeds fill them; Oh, haste,
Ere the sun set, and the summer be past!

What dost thou bring for me, season of bounty,
Autumn,—thy hands overflowing with plenty?

Fruit from the orchard and corn from the field;
Sweet nuts I bring, which the forest trees yield;
Blessings abundant on you I bestow;
What thanks to the heavenly Father you owe!
Ripe fruits I scatter, and frost, on the ground;
Nuts and dry leaves fall together around;
Beautiful blossoms I spread in your way;
Landscapes I show you, as lovely as May;
With bright days and sunny I gladden the heart,
Yet mourn not that soon must their beauty depart.
Enjoy them with thankfulness while they remain,
For soon the cold snow-drifts will cover the plain.

What dost thou bring for me, season austere,—
Hoary-haired Winter? what bringest thou here?

Cold storms I bring; but they soon will be over;
With a mantle of snow the earth's bosom I cover,
But soon it will melt in the sun's smiling beams,
And my bridges of ice will be gone from the streams.
Bright hopes I bring, and sweet pleasures, to cheer
The darkest and stormiest days of the year;
Innocent sports for the gay and the young,
Good books to read, and sweet songs to be sung.

Works, too, I bring you,—good deeds to be done;
Haste to perform them before I am gone.
Let there not be even a short winter day,
Whose hours you have foolishly idled away.

PARNASSUS.

BRIGHTLY the sun is gilding the green peaks
Of the old mountain where the Muses dwelt;
And freshly as in Homer's days of song,
Springs the Castalian fountain by its side,
Bathed in whose waves, the Grecian harp sent forth
Sweet strains, that echo yet in human hearts.

Yet seek no more for inspiration there,
Ye who to fadeless laurel crowns aspire.
Gone from Apollo's consecrated shades,
Long since, their hallowing spirit. By that fount,
So dear to them, ye shall no more descry,
Clad in their leaf and flower-embroidered robes,
The choral sisters. From the Olympian heaven
The gods have vanished, there to rule no more
The childish nations, that with idle faith,
Yielded them homage. Ye shall seek in vain
The winged steed, o'er Beauty's glowing realms,
Fresh with Parnassian dews, to bear you up;

Too weak his pinions for the bolder flights
That Truth's high errands of the seer demand.
Truth from the record book of earth sweeps off
The poet's idle dreams; from Ida's mount
Rolls back the clouds that veiled the fabled seat
Of Jove, and shows the naked mountain top
Kingless and throneless. In sublimer light
Than ever glowed upon Olympus' crest,
Reveals a heaven in which the heroes crowned
With laurel in Elysium would be
But meanest beggars, and its idle gods,
Despised and lifeless images of clay.

All mountains now are holy, and all groves
Are temples, where the humble heart, that loves
To meet with God, may find and worship Him.
One divine spirit breathes in every gale,
Or dwells, in calm repose, wherever blooms
A flower, or waves a tree in living green:
Wherever chants a bird his morning hymn,—
Or whatso'er it be, that may remind
The creature of the infinite Father's power,
Who formed them by his Word, and animates
Their being by his ever present love.
All holy, to the heart that gladly finds
The impress of Almighty wisdom stamped
On every beautiful, every common thing;

And deems that nought that is can be too small,
Too common or too mean, to have no claim
Of kindred with its Maker and our God.

THE DEPARTED.

GONE? Yes, but for a little while the parting and the pain.
Heaven shall restore the near and dear to those they love again.
Gone, whither we shall follow soon, with them the joys to share,
Which for his servants here below, the Lord hath treasured there.

Gone? No: they dwell with us unseen, they share our hopes and fears.
In our rejoicing they rejoice, and sorrow in our tears.
Unseen, God sets his angel watch, with constant care to keep
The ways his children walk by day, and guard their nightly sleep.

Departed, but not dead; yea, more alive than when they dwelt
With us on earth in mortal flesh, and all its weakness felt.
They only lose their earthly part, they gain immortal youth,
Who in the fear of God have lived, and kept his word of truth.

INNOCENCE.

DEAR Innocence in a low cottage dwells,
Where the first sunbeams of the morning kiss
The dew drops from the blossoms, and look in
Through the unshaded windows, wide and fair,
And through her open door; while happiest birds
Sing their spring carols. With her own content,
She never wanders from her home away
To seek for more than Heaven can give her there.
Herself forgetting, with herself at peace,
The morrow can but bring her joy; the night,
That sweet repose remorse can ne'er disturb.
Her seasons have no winter and no frost.
Her garden never fails for fragrant flowers,
Of which she wreathes fresh garlands for the heads
Of infants, whom she watches o'er, and keeps
With all solicitude and tender care;
And whispers in their ears sweet things, which none
Besides can hear, save angels; nor forsakes
Her charge, till they stray wilful from her courts.

Conceit and Folly, Vanity and Pride,
Are blind to every avenue that leads
To her abode; but Wisdom is her guest
By day and night, most honored at her board.
And Mercy and Compassion walk with her;
And Charity and Friendship drink the stream
That issues from the fountain at her gate.
Amid the blossoming roses there she sits,
Unwounded by the thorns: Love shares her seat,
And worships with her in her sanctuary,
And dwells with her through all the season's change.

How happy they who know her voice, and love
Her sweet companionship, and seek for her,
In the warm sunshine of her peaceful home;
And she will call them friends, and give them more
Than they have left behind in palaces.

SPRING FLOWERS.

GATHER me wild flowers, fill my vases full,
Fresh with the dew of morn and breath of Spring.
Fetch me sweet Mayflowers,* that so early dare,
From their close hiding-places to peep forth,

*Epigaca repens, otherwise called Trailing Arbutus.

And deck the earth with beauty, while the snow
Yet lingers in the shadow of the wood:
Bring handfuls of cerulean Innocence,†
That dots the turf all thick with silver stars,
Marsh Marygolds,‡ that make the meadows laugh
With golden sunshine; violets, purple-streaked,
Looking out coyly through their soft-fringed lids;
Deep blue Hepaticas, from sunny slopes
Of wooded hills; gay scarlet Columbines,
That love to nod above the rocky cliff;
Anemones, that hide their blushing heads
Behind green curtains, in the sylvan shade;
Rhodora, that adorns her leafless stems
With crowns of rosy flowers; add graceful bells
Of dog-tooth violets, and white Saxifrage.
Its tale of joy and gladness each shall tell,
And wake old memories of their woodland homes,
Whose floor my feet may never tread again.
Haste, bring them ere they wither in your hands;
Bind them together with a golden thread,
For love, for hope, for memory, and for trust
In Him who made them all so beautiful.

---

†Houstonia, or Oldenlandia Coerulea, a flower extensively found through the United States, and called by various local names, such as Innocence, Venus' Pride and Bluets.

‡This is the proper English name of what is here commonly called Cowslip; in Botany, Caltha palustris.

THE PRICE OF LOVE.

HOW sacred and how dear a trust
  Thou takest with thy marriage vow!
The love which thou hast inly nursed
  Must answer for thee now;

Must teach thy brave and manly heart,
  Her burdens with thine own to bear,
And heaven-descended strength impart,
  To take the double share.

The tender secret of her life,
  Which else from all the world she hides,
The honor of a trusting wife,
  She to thy care confides.

Thine but to love; not thine to make
  A slave or toy; else but a loan
All undeserved; and for her sake
  Thou art but half thine own.

Strong love can no exceptions frame
  To nature's laws; and he must pay

Full price for all that he would claim,
  And give himself away.

Yet richer thus than e'er before,
  Large interest in return he gains,
And finds that Heaven's reward can more
  Than recompense his pains.

NATURE.

WHAT aspects thousand-fold of loveliness
  And grandeur Nature sets before our eyes,
In ever changing sky and blooming earth,
To tempt our admiration and our praise!
Not at rare seasons only,—waited for
Through years of hope and longing,—but as though
She could not be too lavish of her gifts,
Spread all around us daily, so that none
May miss the beauty, who have eyes to see,
Or fail to find the joy, with hearts to feel.
And while the curtains of this earthly tent
She paints with pictures all significant
Of a sublimer life than she can boast,
She wakens, on her thousand-stringed harp,
To charm us, harmonies so deep and full,

That we can utter but a little part
Of what we hear, and ere we comprehend
The depth and fullness, we are raised above
The arms of Nature to a higher sphere.
For Nature's realm is but a theatre,
Whose scenes of beauty and of grandeur stand.
Not only to entrance the wondering eyes,
And fill the heart with rapture, but before
The inner sense to image forth the hand
Of wonder-working power behind the veil.
And to invite and lead us to confess,
The glory is but borrowed from a world
Of life immortal and of light divine;
That what we see is only a reflection—
A shadow of realities unseen:
And Nature, whom we worship as a goddess,
Only a servant of the Lord of all.

SUNSHINE.

SHUT it not out—the golden light,
But let its radiance softly pour
Through the clear window, warm and bright,
Across the yellow floor.

Shut it not out. The joyous sun
Has many a tale to tell to me,
While through the quiet afternoon
His slanted beams I see.

Tales of young years, of childhood's home,
Of Autumn's days,—so calm and clear,
When the warm sunlight used to come
Just as I see it here,

Through windows open to the day,
In that old home, so dear to me,
Whose mossy roof, through far away,
In memory still I see.

Then let the golden sunshine stream
Across my lonely chamber floor;
And let me dream the happy dreams
Of childhood's days once more.

The city's walls that hem me in
Shall seem awhile to fade away,
And hushed shall be its busy din,
As for a Sabbath day.

Tall chestnut groves, with whispering sound,
As when by summer winds caressed,
Shall seem with green to wall me round,
And soothe my heart to rest.

HOME IN THE WOODS.

YE pleasant groves, cool, mossy shadows, green
Retreats of summer, how I mourned your fall!
Gone from the hill-side were the grateful bowers,
The homes of childhood's pleasures, sacred seats
Of its first aspirations after good,
Among whose murmuring leaves the holy voice
That speaks of God in nature, first came down
To one who loved beneath their canopy
To feel the awe of solitude, and breathe
The inspiration of that silent scene.
A little sanctuary in the wood,
Was childhood's home to him, where peacefully
The days and seasons passed, while what is called
"The world" was far removed and all unknown.
The leaves and blossoms were his teachers there,
Reminding him of the creating hand
That fashioned them so wondrously; while books
That echoed their wise teaching, led the way
To fields of wider view, and brought within
Home's dear but narrow circle of delights,
A new companionship:—the wise and good

Of all times and all nations, teach in books,
And we can hear their counsels and give heed,
If we but will. So from beneath the wood
The grown up child went forth, but carried still
The love of forest flowers and forest shades
Within his bosom, while he walked the streets,
Amid the city's busy throng, that seemed
A solitude more lonely than the wood.
And then they hewed the shady groves away,
And let the sunlight in. So Providence
Oft pulls away the bulwarks we have reared
Round some long-cherished object, dear to self,
But shutting out the sunlight from the soul.
So must the bud break open its green cell,
To glow a lovely blossom in the day.
Yet who will not lament, (at least sometimes,)
The fading of the pictures, so endeared,
That curtained childish innocence around,
And kept it, like the wrapped-up bud, awhile,
From the rude contact of the heartless world?

VERSES WRITTEN FOR MR. AND MRS. H

WE are but travellers and pilgrims here,
And a short journey brings us to the end
Of our abode in earthly tabernacles.

When past, at least, how short the time appears!
However wearily and painfully
We trod the marches of the wilderness,
And longed for green oases on the way.
The sun of life has now gone by its noon,
And shadows lengthen, as the sloping rays
Tell of the dark, chill evening soon to come.
Awake, gird up your loins, and be prepared,
When your last earthly day has reached its close,
To welcome the eternal dawn with joy.
Lift up the eyes of Faith even now, and see
The shining tops of the eternal mountains.
How shall earth longer tempt us, when we once
Have seen the glory of their light? what boots
The wealth of India to the traveller, who
To-morrow leaves it for a heritage
Of everlasting worth in heavenly realms.

But you, my friends, need not the poet's song
To inspire your faith, and turn your eyes toward heaven,
While one, who from your household lately passed,
Seems to stand beckoning from beyond the cold
Black stream that parts us from the immortal shore,
Filling your daily thoughts and nightly dreams
With invitations eloquent and sweet,
To follow whither she has gone to dwell.
Nor need you to be taught, that over all

The woes, the wrongs, the wretchedness of earth,
Eternal Mercy sits, disposing all,
And leading those that put their trust in God,
Through all the storms, and all the desert ways
That lie between them and their home in heaven.
And the same mercy takes away, that gives:
And takes an earthly treasure, but to give
One of eternal worth. And we shall know
Hereafter, that He hath done all things well.

Accept, my friends, my Christmas offering:
These verses, which, though they may not contain
Much to instruct or to console, may yet
Afford some pleasure, and a little use
Perform, for friendship's sake, when all without,
Cold Winter's bleak, unfriendly aspect wears.
And if we seldom meet each other here,
Still let us hope that we may stand together,
In the great congregation of the souls
Redeemed from earth, with robes made white and clean,
Immortal brethren, in the Lord's New Heaven.

WRITTEN FOR A LADY BY REQUEST.

THOU askest of my poverty a gift;
Thou askest of my broken harp a song:
Of the disconsolate and the bereft
Thou askest words of comfort for the strong.

Yet I am not so poor as they whose hands
  Are full of gold, without a heart to give.
Let me not grudge their houses and their lands,
  While in sweet peace of conscience I may live.

What shall I say then? He gives best who knows
  That all he has is only lent on trust;
That all, and more than all, to God he owes;
  Nor less, to man, his duty to be just.

Wouldst thou find strength in time of trouble? ask
  Of Him who gives thee all thou call'st thine own,
And with the daily gift, the daily task;
  And leave the morrow to His care alone.

NATURE WORSHIP.

HOW sweet a joy the love of Nature
  Inspired within my youthful breast!
With new delights each blooming feature
  Of her fair face my heart impressed.

How wondrously of Him who made her
  So strangely fair, I thought and felt!
With reverence deeper still and gladder,
  Before the Lord of all I knelt.

Then sweet-voiced Science came to show me
  What mysteries lay in Nature's heart:
In everything above—below me,
  I learned to trace divinest art.

Alas! amid the endless treasures
  Of Nature's ever glorious show,
I quite forgot my noblest pleasure,
  My Maker and myself to know.

The depth of sin, the height of duty,
  The bliss of virtue,—knew I not;
Enchanted by the spell of beauty,
  The hand that gave it I forgot.

With seemingly devout emotion
  I prayed as to a God unknown:
Alas! how vain was my devotion!
  I worshipped but at Nature's throne.

The grove where loving, trustful childhood
  With joy its heavenly Father met,
Became a dank and tangled wildwood
  With chilling dews of error wet.

The flowers that I so dearly cherished
  Faded and withered where they grew;
The sweetness of their odors perished;
  To other groves my song-birds flew.

My heaven with roof of sparkling azure,
  And golden sun, that glowed so bright,
Through childhood's summer hours of pleasure,
  Grew black and stormy to my sight.

Then, when the bow its lovely splendor
  Across the angry storm cloud threw,
And the parched leaves, all fresh and tender,
  Washed by the quickening raindrops, grew,

I recognized the heavenly token,
  And saw with shame, how far my way
Had turned from Him whose Word had spoken
  Fair Nature into life and day;—

From Him without whose heart-felt presence,
  All outward joys are fleeting things:
And only humble, meek obedience
  Enduring peace and blessing brings.

YOUTH AND AGE.

STAY with me, Youth, I cried, and fill me up
  The measure of thy beauty and thy bliss.
Prolong thy cool and fragrant morning hours:
Keep fresh the dewy blossoms of thy prime.

Let not the promises which thou hast made
Of good to come, prove vain and flattering dreams.
Leave me not yet to wrinkles and grey hairs.

But Youth replied, I may not stay with thee.
Unless I leave thee, Wisdom cannot come:
And she hath better gifts for thee than mine.
My joys are but as feasts at wayside inns;
Hers, the delights of dear and happy home,
After the journey and the toil are past.
Unless my blossoms fade away and die,
No fruit shall ripen for thy Autumn store,
No harvest for thy Winter's bread be reaped.

So Youth departed; and so Age came on;
My brow was wrinkled and my head grew grey.
And Wisdom,—where was she? I cannot tell.
With senses dulled and numbed, decrepit limbs,
And shattered memory, I can but wait,
Hoping to see my silver purged from dross,
The chaff and tares all winnowed from my wheat,
When I have laid mortality aside.

AFFLICTIONS, BLESSINGS IN DISGUISE.

AS above the darkest storm-cloud
Shines the sun, serenely bright,

Waiting to restore to Nature
  All the glory of his light,

So, behind each cloud of sorrow,
  So, in each affliction, stands
Hid, an angel, with a blessing
  From the Father in his hands.

As without the tempest, pouring
  O'er the earth the welcome rain,
All were but a fruitless desert,
  Barren sand for ripening grain,

So, if ne'er a cloud of sadness
  Veiled the sunshine of the soul,—
If affliction's waves were never
  Suffered o'er the heart to roll,—

Love and faith might fail forever
  To bring forth their fruits of peace;
Heaven's good seed of truth would perish
  In a thorny wilderness.

So, with cloud and storm and tempest
  Grows our earthly summer dim,
That the rebel heart, our Father
  Thus may win to turn to Him.

And like Israel's tribes, we wander
  In the desert, waste and drear,

Hungering, thirsting, faint and weary,
Month by month and year by year,

There we taste the wondrous manna,
Heavenly food by angels brought:
Quench our thirsting at the fountain
Of the rock which Moses smote;

Till, (how late!) we learn the lesson,
Not by bread alone we live,
But by every word of blessing
Which the mouth of God doth give.

WHAT HAST THOU THOUGHT OF DEATH.

WHAT hast thou thought of Death?
To lie enshrouded in the clay-cold cell,
With kindred worms unconsciously to dwell,
When thou dost yield thy breath?

Hast thou before thine eye
The pallid corpse, the cold sepulchral stone,
The mouldering dust, the bleached and fleshless bone?
Who would not dread to die!

Oh, put this gloom away!
Leave, with the spirit, in its heavenward flight,

This dark abode; let thy thoughts dwell in light,—
In glory,—not in clay.

The insect's radiant wings,—
The blossoms thou hast planted o'er the tomb,
To deck the spot with consecrated bloom,—
Shall teach thee better things.

Let the light odorous flower
Lift thy thoughts upward from the darksome earth,
Whence its gay petals and fresh leaves had birth,
With unresisted power.

The crawling worm that wakes
Anew to winged life in summer air,
Forgets at once the sordid birth-place, where
The narrow cell he breaks.

Forget thou thus the tomb,
As they, who leave its darkness far behind,
And in the fragrant heavenly gardens bind
Wreath of immortal bloom.

And glimpses of their light,
Like coming morning radiance, shall illume
The clouds that hangs Death's narrow way with gloom,
Even to thy mortal sight.

THE MAPLE TREE.

UNDER the Maple in early Spring,
When first the blue-bird begins to sing!
See him! he's perched on the topmost spray:
He's thinking of building a nest some day.

Under the Maple on the hill,
Over the brook that turns the mill;
It stands by itself, and overlooks
The village, the cornfields, the meadows and brooks.

Wide it stretched its knotty arms,
Pointing each way o'er the neighbor's farms;
Its trunk is larger than you and I
Could reach around, if we both should try.

Under the Maple all red with bloom,
Come, when the south wind is blowing; come
When the sky is blue, and the golden ray
Of the April sunshine is warm as May.

Sweet is the scent of the Maple flower.
When the fields are brown and leafless the bower:
And the violet buds are sleeping still
In their snug green chambers beside the hill.

Come for a nosegay to-day; for few
Are the days in April so warm and blue;
To-morrow, the cold north-east may blow,
With its clouds and rain, with its sleet and snow.

Under the Maple again! 'Tis May;
And the little blue butterfly's out at play;
There are field flowers now, and the busy bee
Has begun her work for the Spring, you see.

The maple blossoms are gone; but now
Green leaf-buds are bursting on every bough:
And the thrush and the robin are singing with glee
Among the limbs of the Maple tree.

The gladdest sunshine of all the year
Falls when the fresh green lea· es appear,
And twinkles and flashes from every spray.
As the soft May winds with the branches play.

Under the Maple when Summer has come,
With her clover-fields sweet and her roses in bloom:
And the leaves are so green and so thick overhead.
Like a tent in the summer heat outspread.

When the sun is high and the sky is clear,
The farmer's cattle that pasture near,
Love to come and lie down in the shade,
So cool and green, by the maple made.

And the nests of the birds are so snugly hid
The clustering maple-boughs amid,
That the sharpest eyes in vain will look
For the shining eggs in their leafy nook.

Under the Maple when Autumn is here,
Come, when the sky is bright and clear,
And the forests, like royal tents, are spread
With curtains of purple and gold and red.

And the Maple tree, with his crimson crown,
Looks on the white, ripe cornfields down:
And the pale wild asters, white and blue.
Bend with the heavy Autumn dew.

Come while 'tis sunny and warm and bright.
And the fields look glad in the mellow light;
For the cold, black frost will soon be here,
With death to each blossom so sweet and dear.

And the storm-wind will scatter all thick around,
The rosy leaves on the frosted ground;
And the maple boughs will swing gaunt and bare,
In the sullen gusts of the wintry air.

BEYOND THE GATE.

I KNOW the way is rough and weary;
The evening clouds look dark and dreary,
That gather where we sit and wait:
But every moment brings us nearer
A morning where the sky is clearer,
A brighter home than this, and dearer;
And there is rest beyond the gate.

One Winter more has just passed o'er us:
Another Spring lies close before us,
With promise sweet of song and bloom.
O childish joy in vernal flowers!
How oft the chilling tempest lowers
O'er Spring's green fields and budding bowers,
And shades the sunny day with gloom!

But in that happier country whither
We turn our eyes, no storm-clouds gather,
Nor frosts the tender bloom destroy.
Into thy fold, Good Shepherd, lead us:
In green and heavenly pastures feed us;
Safe through the lonely journey speed us,
Home to the mansions of thy joy.

WHAT HAVE I DONE.

WHAT have I done!
With retrospect as honest as I can,
My brief day's work attentively I scan.
What deeds of love to God, or good to man?
Low in the West I see the setting sun;
What have I done?

What have I done,
To cause me joy that such a chance was given
To take yet one step further on towards heaven?
What done amiss, that needs to be forgiven?
Bear witness for me, O departing sun;
What have I done?

What have I done?
'Tis all recorded in the eternal book;
Who without dread upon its leaves may look?
I must give up again the charge I took.
How have I done, O conscience, let me ask,
This earthly task.

'Tis almost done;
Father, thou knowest whether well or ill;
If I in anything have done thy will.
What can I more, my errand to fulfil,
Ere the last sands of ebbing life are run?
'Twill soon be done.

AUTUMN.

SO Autumn, thou art come!
I love the mildness of thine early breath,
So gently whispering, as it tells the death
Of lovely Summer's bloom.
Yet thou hast thine own flowers
All thickly scattered by the traveller's way;
Lavish of purple and of gold are they;
While all the forest bowers
Will soon be gaily dressed
In many-colored garments,—richer far
Than coronation robes of monarchs are.
And then will sink to rest
The leaves and blossoms down
To mother earth; and we will not lament
The fading of that beauty, only lent
To garnish Autumn's crown.

'Tis soft and balmy now,
Like Spring in Italy, as poets tell;
As though the south wind had a magic spell,
To deck the green hills' brow
Again with vernal gems,
To bid the sere leaf freshen on the tree,
And birds renew their May-time jubilee
Amid the blossoming stems.
Vain dream! Enjoy awhile
The enchanted scene; witch-hazel blossoms pale
A little longer scent the Autumnal gale,
And blue fringed gentians smile
To the October sun,
A lonely aster here and there remains,
Till keener frosts and cold November rains
Have vanquished every one.

MESSIAH.

WHEN o'er the earth a fearful night its veil of darkness spread,
And scarce a single trembling star its feeble lustre shed,
To light the path that here and there a lonesome traveller trod,
Who sought, with slow and doubtful step, the temple of his God,—

When over almost every eye had fallen the sleep of death,
And cheerless and forlorn, the weary nations sat beneath
The clouds of darkness that concealed the light which once had shone
Upon the earth with glory long forgotten and unknown,—
A voice came from the wilderness, "Prepare, prepare the way
For Him who comes to bring again the light of heavenly day;
Before Him let the mountains bow; each crooked way make straight;
Exalt the valleys where he comes to enter Zion's gate.
Repent ye, for the harvest time of all the earth is near;
The Husbandman to gather in His sheaves will soon appear:
Repent, and bring forth worthy fruits for Him who comes to see
If there be grapes upon his vine or figs upon his tree."
So taught the appointed messenger, who, as Elias, came,
The advent of the Son of God in Israel to proclaim.
Hear, Judah! hear, Jerusalem! the glad announcement hear!
The prophet ye have waited for will soon on earth appear.
The promised heir to David's throne, your Saviour and your king,
To the imprisoned and the bound deliverance comes to bring;
Strength to the feeble he shall give, and soundness to the lame:
The sick and wounded shall be healed; the dumb confess his name;
The deaf and heavy ear, unstopped, rejoice to hear his word;
The blind, with open eyes, shall see the glory of the Lord.

Peace, not heaven-born, but as of death, reigned o'er the
waiting earth,
In that dark hour which gave the long-desired Messiah birth:
As though the powers of hell had thought that all was overcome,
The last good angel fled, so Eden now might be their home;
And having laid aside their arms and warfare for a while,
Sat down upon the ruined world to rest and share the spoil.
Then came the Lord of glory down, to bring salvation near,
That men, who were about to die, his living word might hear.
He veiled his glory in a cloud, that mortal eyes might see
His face and live, who came from sin and death to set them free.
He came, but not with regal pomp, and not with martial train,
Deliverance from the Roman yoke for Israel's sons to gain;
Not to exalt the proud in heart, who dared, with impious
praise,
To flatter Him who from the heavens beheld their crooked
ways.
Their fathers bowed to wood and stone, and with the prophets' blood,
Whose word they would not hear, defiled the land on which
they stood;
Yet, unrepented and unwept their fathers' deeds of shame,
With solemn rite and lip devout, they invoked Jehovah's
name,
And vainly dreamed that to their race he would again restore
The majesty and kingdom to be theirs forevermore;
Yea, that himself, as David's son, on David's throne should sit,

And all the world should there bestow their honors at his feet.

He came—but they who had despised his prophets and his word,
Refused to own him as their King, to adore him as their Lord;
They saw not in his humble guise, his meek and sorrowful face,
The love which stooped to seek the lost and win the rebel race:
And though they saw him heal the sick and cause the dead to live,
Acknowledged not his power divine, the sinner to forgive;
But with an impious scorn ascribed to demons from below,
The glory which a God alone upon him could bestow.
An outlawed miscreant's release, instead of his, they claim,
And give him to a felon's death of agony and shame.
Earth, fear and tremble, for the deeds that are upon thee done!
Veil thee with night and be ashamed, O thou astonished sun!
Wonder and be amazed, O heavens, at guilt so deep and dread!—
At mercy so divine and large, that bows the Saviour's head
All patiently to shame and death—to death that he may take
Immortal power, the bars of death forevermore to break.
Rejoice ye saints and shout, for your deliverer is at hand!
The Captain of the heavenly hosts, almighty to command,
Has fought with death and conquered hell, and now ascends to reign
In heaven, and there the throne of truth forever to maintain:

Forever to defend and save, with his right hand of might.
All those that put their trust in him and in his law delight.

THE WEARY WAY.

O HOLLOW, soulless pomp which decks
  The sordid pageants that pass by,
While the sad heart with longing breaks,
  For food which can its needs supply.

Nothing this emptiness can fill
  But bread of heaven; naught that thirst
Can quench, but the refreshing rill
  Which 'neath the tree of life doth burst.

Hungering and thirsting, on we wend
  Our dark and solitary way,
Knowing not where our steps to bend,
  But longing for the dawn of day.

In storm and weariness we tread
  Our path of sorrow, while around
False lights their meteor lustre shed,
  Eyes dim with watching to confound.

We falter,—fall; an angel's hand
  Lifts us; an angel's voice we hear:

"Mercy shall guide you to the land
  Of heavenly rest—be of good cheer."

Our Lord is always near to save,
  When least of all we feel his power;
Even the dark midnight of the grave
  He makes a joyful triumph hour.

For then our everlasting home
  We find, where sighing and distress,
And night and darkness, cannot come;
  But the bright sun of Righteousness

Shall bless us with eternal day,
  All in its noontide light revealed,
For which we now but hope and pray;—
  The fount of heaven's delight unsealed.

TO DR. DEAN'S EAGLE.

PROUD bird of freedom! ah, is this your fate,
To lurk about the Doctor's barn and wait
For whatsoever comes within your way,
Whether 'tis lawful or unlawful prey?
They say you clear the yard of mice and rats,
And sometimes pounce upon unlucky cats,
And though unable to procure the dish

Yourself, you like to dine or sup on fish.
Like a dilapidated turkey, there
You stand and meditate on what you were,
When you were able to enjoy the fun
Of soaring high, and looking at the sun,
Of going out a-fishing when you please,
And roosting nightly on the tallest trees;
Not even dreaming that a broken wing
Such sad disgrace upon your pride would bring,
And hold you bound, spite of your noble birth,
A hapless prisoner close to mother earth.
But I am much afraid you have no claim,
At least no just one, to the praise and fame
Bestowed upon you in orations, made
With less regard for truth than for parade;
Or song of poets, crammed with flattering lies
About "Jove's bird," the favorite of the skies.
In fact, I don't believe a single word
Of what the poets say, you ugly bird,
About your greatness. My opinion is,
(With due regard for personalities,)
That of all feathered fowl that ever flew,
There can't be found a meaner thief than you.
Others, besides me, think 'twas a mistake,
When Uncle Sam decided you to take
To be his armor-bearer. But, you see,
Rome had the eagle, therefore, so must we.
But of this matter there's another view,

Which makes it quite appropriate that you,
In your capacity should represent
A bold, audacious, thievish government,
Which once made prey of Texas, and which would
Steal Canada and Cuba, if it could.
I don't assert this latter view is just;
But those who like can take it, upon trust.
And now, perhaps you'll think I've said enough:
So good-by to your eagleship: I'm off.

THE APPLE TREE.

SOME praise the oak with its branches of iron,
That weathers the storms of a century through,
And still seems as fresh as when only a sapling,
It stood in spring garments all verdant and new.

And some praise the laurel, whose green boughs o'ershadow
The foreheads of poets and nobles and braves;
And some the chaste willow, so gracefully drooping,
That weeps in sad beauty o'er tear-hallowed graves.

And some the green cedar of Lebanon honor,
So noble a tree and so worthy of fame,
Which the wisest of monarchs in Israel once hallowed,
A temple to build to Jehovah's great name.

But let me to a tree of more humble pretensions,
  Though none the less useful, give honor in verse;
The tree of the household, the pride of the orchard,—
  The apple tree's praises I fain would rehearse.

The sweet blooming apple-tree, motherly apple-tree:—
  What a rich burden in Autumn it bears;
Not like the pine or the ash or the cedar,
  Lifting their fruitless tops up toward the stars,

But spreading so widely its well-laden branches,
  With fruit for man's using all humbly it stands,
And asks but for hearts that are filled with thanksgiving
  For the gifts it brings forth from Heaven's bountiful hands.

Come, join with me then in the apple-tree's praises,
  So worthy, and yet how neglected in song!
While the rose, charming only by perishing beauty,
  Is sung by all poets, extolled by each tongue.

Yet the apple-tree's bloom is as lovely in Spring-time,
  And sweet as the rose that the poets extol;
While the rose-bush, in view of the fruit-laden orchard,
  In Autumn stands lone and neglected by all.

CHRISTMAS VERSES FOR A NEW CHURCH MINISTER.

O COLD and cheerless Winter night,
  That gave the babe of Bethlehem birth!
O welcome, host of angels bright,
  That sing of love and peace on earth!
O welcome, heavenly star, that tells
Where the descended Saviour dwells!

Go, servant of your Lord: proclaim
  The joyful message far and wide:
Salvation in the wondrous name
  Of him who bore the cross and died,
And burst the bondage of the grave,
And rose with power divine to save.

Go, preach that all the painted lies
  That cover guilt and wrong to-day,
Hypocrisy's and crime's disguise,
  Shall by and by be swept away;
And Truth's glad morning, clear and bright,
Dispel the shades of Winter night.

Go, prophesy the Spring-time near,
  The Summer day of Love at hand,
When earth's broad fields shall bloom and bear
  A heavenly harvest, and the land
Which war defiled with blood-stains, be
Green with the peaceful olive tree.

SIMILITUDES.

PHILOSOPHER, who in the calm sublime
  Of meditation, on the mountain top
Dost sit, descend; and if upon the heaven
Which thou hast dwelt so near, thou may'st have read
A truth which it were good for us to love,
Bring it, and labor with us in the work
Of making it our own and thine forever.

The sunlight silvers o'er the mountain peaks
With heaven-like splendor; but the upper air
Which fans their bald acclivities, is chill
With frost of endless winter; and the clouds
Which girdle them around with shining belts,
Float there on icy wings, and scatter snows
And biting hail out from their fleecy folds;
But when they seek the vales below, dissolve
In genial showers, or pour in rivulets down

The mountain side, to water all the mead,
And bless the labors of the tiller's hand.
Then first the crystal waters feel the glow
Of the warm sun, beneath whose golden beams
Unveiled, they seemed, in clouds, to hang so near.

Nor shall the truth on which thou dost but gaze,
As on the breaking of the morning o'er
The purpled tops of distant mountains, be
Filled with the warmth of love, till thou hast learned
To use it in love's service. It shall then
Be wings for thee, to bear thee onward still
To fields of new delight: and thou shalt warm
The life-blood of thy spirit with the toil
Of joyous flight, and gather, like the bee,
Celestial nectar from each earth-born flower.

And the gay hues with which the sunbeam paints
The floating clouds, that margin round the tent
Of heaven, are like imagination's dreams,—
Forever changing with the changing hours.
But when the clouds pour down their watery stores,
And the glad sun looks forth, behold the bow,
That binds the changing colors to the form
Of heavenly order, as the Maker's hand
Once placed them, when he blessed the earth anew,
And gave the world the promise of his grace.

THE WILD FLOWERS.

PALE blossoms, ye appear
Not in the pageant hues,
Nor with the fragrant breath,
The garden's favorites bear;
But silently the dews,
On the untrodden heath,
Into your small bells pour the trembling tear.

How sweetly do ye look,
When breathes the warm south wind
Upon the budding earth,
From every sunlit nook,
Where close ye lay enshrined,
Rejoicing to come forth,
And smile by hill-side, meadow, bank and brook.

Ye make the solitude
Glad, as ye cluster there;
And gracefully ye bend
In green and lonely wood,

And through the summer air
Your faint, sweet odors send
From every spot which Spring with beauty hath renewed.

Ye are like those who dwell
Far from the busy crowd,
To whom the books of fame
Are sealed; yet who can tell
Of sweetest joys bestowed
By conscience void of blame,
Of peace earth cannot give, nor all its storms dispel.

TO-DAY AND TO-MORROW.

ANOTHER year is added to the sum
Of years that measure our brief sojourn here.
Like and yet various, as they swiftly pass.
Each changing season brings its hopes and fears,
Its cares and labors, its delights and joys.
But oft, the sorrows and the cares appear
To outweigh the joys and the delights we find:
And we grow weary of the tiresome round
Of labors, seeming endlessly the same.
Step after step secures no new advance;
No happier prospect opens with the dawn
Of the new day: year after year glides by.

And leaves us at the end as far removed
From what we toiled and labored most to gain,
As at the first. How mean a thing! sayest thou,
What wretchedness is life! But think again.
Hast thou no treasures of experience gained?
No wisdom from the lessons of the year,
Which Providence has set as in a book
Before thee? Hast thou never raised thy sight
Above the earth on which thy footsteps rest;
Nor looked beyond the narrow lines which bound
The acres of thy father's heritage,—
Beyond the horizon of this mortal sphere,
Which thou must soon forsake? Forsake for what?
Learn, if thou hast not learned, that thou art here
Only a scholar in the art of life:
The eternal morrow shall thy freedom be,
Where thou shalt gather and enjoy the fruit
Of all thy toil, if thou hast learned aright,
And wisely done the duties of to-day.
But if, like idle, truant scholars, thou
Hast loitered all away thy golden hours,
And played at hide and seek with Folly, while
Thou should'st have companied with Wisdom, what
Reward but that of Folly canst thou hope?

CHARITY.

DESCEND, celestial charity, and breathe,
With thy reviving warmth, upon a world
Of wretchedness and woe, that knows thee not.
Wake its lethargic slumberers from the dreams
That steal their reason, and delude their sense
With selfish fantasies and idle hopes;
Wake them to see thy loveliness, to feel
Thy power to bless, and own thou art divine.
Breathe, as the south wind breathes in time of Spring,
On the cold winter scene that sin hath made
Of Eden's blooming garden, and release
From the stern bondage of the frost the streams
That watered it, and send them forth again
Upon their joyous errand. Let thy smile
Visit the desolate and leafless bowers
Of Paradise, and from the slumbering buds
The gentle dews and rains of heaven shall call
The tender leaves, and bid the fragrant flowers
With promise of celestial fruit expand.

Then from their distant pilgrimage the birds
Shall come, and build among the verdant boughs,
And sing their loves, and fill the vernal woods
With hymns of joy and gladness. Then again
Man shall return and dwell there, and shall see
To read in every green and living thing,
The name of Him who formed it, and shall hear
In all the songs, "the Lord Jehovah liveth."

THE TEMPTATION.

An imitation or free translation of Schiller's poem, entitled "Sehnsucht." (Longing.)

HOW lovely in the sunlight stand
The green hills of the blessed land!
What heavenly peaceful music strains
Gladden its happy groves and plains!

O how refreshing is the air
That breathes upon the dwellers there!
What fragrances the zephyrs bring
From gardens of immortal Spring!

What rich balsamic fruits are seen
Glowing amid the youthful green,

The freshness of whose summer hour
Fears no destroying Winter's power!

O that those blissful bowers might be
A shelter and a home for me!
Had I but wings, those hills of light
Should soon arrest my eager flight.

Vain wish! no wings could bear thee o'er
The seas which part thee from that shore.
On its fierce billows thou must ride;
The beating of its storms abide.

Yet venture boldly. They alone
Who venture life, win Virtue's crown.
She gives no pledge; no faithless heart
Finds in her paradise a part.

CONTENTS.

www.ingramcontent.com/pod-product-compliance
Lightning Source LLC
Chambersburg PA
CBHW030616270326
41927CB00007B/1201
9783744704854